Become.

Become.

by Emery Allen

© 2013 Emery Allen

All rights reserved. No part of this book may be used or reproduced in any form without written permission from the author except in the case of brief quotations.

Cover and internal photographs by Emery Allen © 2013

ISBN 978-1-312-25647-7

Self published in the USA with international distribution.

For everyone on the verge of being.

You're the vastness and the galaxies.
You constantly remind me
that the sun is
worth saving.

You are the Mississippi River.
How many people have you cleansed?
Who has laughed in you? Loved in you?
Is it lonely to only be flowing?
To never stay long enough
to be cleansed in return?
How much do you take with you
when you leave?
How many people have put their faith in you,
let you carry it somewhere they've never been?
Who has leaned into you,
eyes closed,
whispering their deepest secrets?
Did they ask if you were sad?
Did they dip their fingers in
and listen when you said,
"Yes, this is where it hurts.
This is where it all happened.
Do you know where I've been?
Do you know what I've seen?"

Your higher self exists
in a drop of water.
The ocean misses you.
Can't you feel it pulling?

Dear future me,

    Don't be afraid to love again. Don't let the cracks in your heart turn to scars. I hope you laugh every day. I hope you feel beautiful. I hope you make others smile. Remember that you don't need many people, and don't lower yourself so you'll have more. Be strong when things get tough. Remember that the universe is always doing what's best for you. Recognize when you're wrong and learn from it. Don't hold on too tightly. Always look back and see how much you've grown. Be proud of yourself. Don't change for anyone. Give more. Give the things you love so others can love them too. Write stories. Take photos. Remember moments and the way certain people look at you. Be you. Keep growing. Keep going.

Love,
me

(I dreamt you were
a flower in my hands.
I watched you die
and I wept for you.)

forgive & let go forgive & let go forgive & let go
forgive & let go forgive & let go forgive & let go
forgive & let go forgive & let go forgive & let go
forgive & let go forgive & let go forgive & let go
forgive & let go forgive & let go forgive & let go
forgive & let go forgive & let go forgive & let go
forgive & let go forgive & let go forgive & let go
forgive & let go forgive & let go forgive & let go
forgive & let go forgive & let go forgive & let go
forgive & let go forgive & let go forgive & let go
forgive & let go forgive & let go forgive & let go
forgive & let go forgive & let go forgive & let go
forgive & let go forgive & let go forgive & let go
forgive & let go forgive & let go forgive & let go
forgive & let go forgive & let go forgive & let go
forgive & let go forgive & let go forgive & let go
forgive & let go forgive & let go forgive & let go
forgive & let go forgive & let go forgive & let go
forgive & let go forgive & let go forgive & let go
forgive & let go forgive & let go forgive & let go
forgive & let go forgive & let go forgive & let go
forgive & let go forgive & let go forgive & let go
forgive & let go forgive & let go forgive & let go
forgive & let go forgive & let go forgive & let go
forgive & let go forgive & let go forgive & let go
forgive & let go forgive & let go forgive & let go
forgive & let go forgive & let go forgive & let go
forgive & let go forgive & let go forgive & let go
forgive & let go forgive & let go forgive & let go

forgive & let go forgive & let go forgive & let go
forgive & let go forgive & let go forgive & let go
forgive & let go forgive & let go forgive & let go
forgive & let go forgive & let go forgive & let go
forgive & let go forgive & let go forgive & let go
forgive & let go forgive & let go forgive & let go
forgive & let go forgive & let go forgive & let go
forgive & let go forgive & let go forgive & let go
forgive & let go forgive & let go forgive & let go
forgive & let go forgive & let go forgive & let go
forgive & let go forgive & let go forgive & let go
forgive & let go forgive & let go forgive & let go
forgive & let go forgive & let go forgive & let go
forgive & let go forgive & let go forgive & let go
forgive & let go forgive & let go forgive & let go
forgive & let go forgive & let go forgive & let go
forgive & let go forgive & let go forgive & let go
forgive & let go forgive & let go forgive & let go
forgive & let go forgive & let go forgive & let go
forgive & let go forgive & let go forgive & let go
forgive & let go forgive & let go forgive & let go
forgive & let go forgive & let go forgive & let go
forgive & let go forgive & let go forgive & let go
forgive & let go forgive & let go forgive & let go
forgive & let go forgive & let go forgive & let go
forgive & let go forgive & let go forgive & let go
forgive & let go forgive & let go forgive & let go
forgive & let go forgive & let go forgive & let go

(AUGUST)
the month you forget.
the month it stops hurting.
the month the heat kisses you
and leaves your skin wet.
the month of Queen Anne's Lace.
the month you feel empty.
the month a stranger tells you he loves you
and you don't know what that means.

this is where you are.
this is where you wake up.
this is where you remember.

I wanted
    to stay.

He wanted to
    sit around with your heart.

He is not a constellation.
You should not wish to be
the cigarette touching his lips.
He will not appear through the fog
and heal your wounds.
Only you can do that.
So get out of bed and put some lipstick on.
Stop falling at his feet.
Save yourself.

An artist should not fall in love with another artist.
A poet should not fall in love with another poet.
Play it safe. It's easier that way.
Kiss people who can't understand
why you cry when the sun sets,
who think it is because you're afraid of the dark.

Don't shrink in her hands.

Your soul is an ocean.

What I meant to say was
love someone who leaves so many fucking holes in you
that if they were to walk away,
half of your soul would go with them.

I'm trying to love people because they exist and not because of what they can do for me.

I'll catch your tears in a mason jar
and kiss your scars until they turn into waves.
When the time is right,
I'll carry you and your salty water to the beach
and we'll lay with the tides
until you feel like you're home again.

Having
too much love in me
is a silly reason
to be
sad.

But where
am I supposed to put it?

There's so much more to life than finding someone who will want you, or being sad over someone who doesn't. There's a lot of wonderful time to be spent discovering yourself without hoping someone will fall in love with you along the way, and it doesn't need to be painful or empty. You need to fill yourself up with love. Not anyone else. Become a whole being on your own. Go on adventures, fall asleep in the woods with friends, wander around the city at night, sit in a coffee shop on your own, write on bathroom stalls, leave notes in library books, dress up for yourself, give to others, smile a lot. Do all things with love, but don't romanticize life like you can't survive without it. Live for yourself and be happy on your own. It isn't any less beautiful, I promise.

Be kind to yourself while blooming.
I know sometimes it feels
like your soul doesn't always fit.
It's all a part of the process.

Letting go is such a difficult thing to understand. Trying to let go is like trying not to think about something. You're just going to think about it even more. I think letting go is less of an ending of one thing and more of an acceptance of everything. It's okay that this is the way it is right now. There's no other way it's supposed to be.

I feel like a part of my soul has loved you since the beginning of everything.

Maybe we're from the same star.

When
nobody else
will love you,

love yourself.

Be patient with yourself. You grow at the rate you are meant to grow. You heal at the rate you are meant to heal. Have faith in yourself. Even when you're lying on the floor of the shower sobbing. Even when you can't get out of bed for weeks. Even when you're afraid to answer the phone. Have faith in yourself. You are given what you can handle, you have the strength to go on. And you are here for a reason. I hope you know that. And I hope you hold on to the forever burning light ahead of you (I know it is so difficult to see sometimes but it is waiting for you). You were not made for the darkness.

Loss is inevitable. Cry when they go. Whisper to them through the stars. And instead of letting loss scar you and make you hide from the ones you love in fear of losing them too, love them even more. Appreciate the small moments shared. Let death be a reminder that this life is not long and that you must reach out and grab something if you truly want it. Be honest, be raw, be forgiving. Know that when your loved ones leave, they are not really gone. Death is nothing more than a transition. They will visit you in your dreams, in feathers, in knocks on the window, in closing doors. You carry parts of their soul with you eternally.

Do not look at another person with judgment in your heart. Let jealousy come and let it go. Love them because they are lucky enough to have the beautiful things that you desire. Bless them. Do not look down on someone for gossiping, for speaking harshly, for causing pain, for hating. The ones who are hurting do not understand how to feel their own pain choose to inflict it on others. It is not a characteristic of an evil spirit but a struggling one. So when someone is mean, remember the pain you can't see inside of them and love them. Forgive them for their actions. Forgive them for their words. Love them.

When someone walks away from you, do not beg them to stay. Do not hold on to their ankles hoping it will stop them. Let them keep walking. Beautiful things will not always last and it is okay. You will be okay. If your heart is full of them, let it remain that way. Love them through the leaves, through the people you interact with, through the moments alone, through unsent letters. Some people make homes in our hearts and it is difficult to tear them down. Let them leave anyways. If they are for you, only time can tell. Keep going.

Let it go.
Nothing is real,
we only exist for a small amount of time.
Everything happens for a reason.
Be easy.
Love where you are.
Love all things around you.

And please,
let it go.

You
are
the
door,
the
path,
and
the
light.

Not everything is supposed to become something beautiful and long lasting. Sometimes people come into your life to show you what is right and what is wrong, to how you who you can be, to teach you to love yourself, to make you feel better for a little while, or to just be someone to walk with at night and spill your life to. Not everyone is going to stay forever, and we still have to keep on going and thank them for what they've given us.

Graphite covered rug,
graphite covered rabbit paws,
art within itself.
Cold everything.
Wet silence.
Soft existence,
like a flower petal,
like a foggy ghost that walks by your door
every morning to say hello.
Loud words no sound
(and isn't that the way it goes?)
Blue knots.
Pink cracking lips.
The tongue does nothing.
Did you say something?
Should I wait for you to?
I didn't think so.
Melting worlds on windshields.
Puddles on the verge of freezing.
Human doings on the verge of being.
We're all on the verge of loving.

Welcome to today.

I am sorry
if I
ever contributed
to the
suffering
of your
heart.

      I dreamt
           I fell in love
   and
turned into a constellation.

If you are feeling empty,
go watch a flower
until you feel like crying
because of how astonishingly beautiful
its simple existence is.
Then watch it a little longer.
Practice being that flower.

I'm often difficult to love. I go through dark periods like the moon and hide from myself. But I promise I will kiss your wounds when they're hurting. Even if they're in your soul, I can find them with the light in my fingertips. I will lead you to the river so you can remember how beautiful it feels to be moved by something that is out of your control. And when our dark periods match, we can breathe with the grass and look at the night sky. The stars will remind us of the beauty in our struggles and we won't feel lost anymore.

Bring me warm rain
and lavender
and you.
I want you most of all.

You don't need another human being
to make your life complete,
but let's be honest.
Having your wounds kissed
by someone who doesn't seem them as
disasters in your soul
but cracks to put their love into
is the most calming thing in this world.

Rules of Autumn:

- Kiss the leaves before they show you their true colors.
- Study your fingerprints until you find out your history.
- Smile at every stranger.
- Go deep inside yourself until you get to the spinning light. Stay there.
- Thank a tree for your breath.
- Knit a scarf made of the things you wish you said this Summer. Give it to someone who will wrap it tightly around his heart for when it gets cold.
- Watch the sunrise. Pretend you are the sun.
- Study your palm lines until you find out your future.
- Be the trees that lose their leaves. Die from your old self. You will bloom again in the spring. You always do.

I'm pointing at my heart
and speaking of you.

Kiss your own fingertips
and hug your own curves.
You are made of waves and honey
and spicy peppers when it is necessary.
You are a goddess,
I hope you haven't forgotten.

I wonder if our fingerprints
fill each other's empty spaces
when we put our hands together.
I want our bodies to move life flowers opening.
Are you afraid of the vastness of the universe
or the humble ones inside of your bloodstream?
When you walk outside in the middle of the night
and it's snowing and it's fifteen degrees,
do you run to your car
or do you stop for a moment to smile at the sky?
Have you reached the peak of the mountain?
Is it everything you'd hoped it would be?
I think if we were trees we'd be willows
and we'd let children swing on our branches.
I'm whispering into the air hoping you will hear me:
Your soul is my soul's home.

I think I fall in love a little bit
with anyone who shows me their soul.
This world is so guarded and fearful.
I appreciate rawness so much.

You embody
the energy of the full moon
and you glow just the same.

You are always burning
and I am always open.
And I fan your flames to make you stronger,
to make you aware of your own existence
and the beauty behind every burnt tree.
You are falling,
you are crashing,
you are turning to ash.
And I know that it hurts,
but this is how it feels to discover yourself.
You are on the ground
and you feel like you are nothing.
This is where it happens.
Do you feel your roots?
Do you see the sun?
You are not alone in this dirt.
The pain is just showing you that you are alive.
It is time to start over
and grow the way you've always wanted to.
It is time to become.

Made in the USA
San Bernardino, CA
03 January 2018